ANDRE BUSTANOBY

WHEN YOUR MATE
IS NOT A
CHRISTIAN

PYRANEE
BOOKS

Zondervan Publishing House
Grand Rapids, Michigan

When Your Mate Is Not a Christian
Copyright © 1989 by Andre Bustanoby

Pyranee Books
are published by
Zondervan Publishing House
1415 Lake Dr., S.E.
Grand Rapids, MI 49506

Library of Congress Cataloging-in-Publication Data

Bustanoby, André.
    When your mate is not a Christian / by Andre Bustanoby.
       p. cm.
    "Pyranee books."
    ISBN 0-310-44371-7
    1. Interfaith marriage—United States. 2. Marriage—Religious aspects—Christianity. I. Title.
    HQ1031.B82 1989   88–34040
    306.8'43—dc19   CIP

Unless otherwise noted, Scripture quotations are taken from the *Holy Bible: New International Version* (North American Edition), copyright © 1973, 1978, 1984 by The International Bible Society. Used by permission of Zondervan Bible Publishers.

THE STORIES IN THIS BOOK ARE TRUE. THE NAMES HAVE BEEN CHANGED EXCEPT FOR REFERENCES TO THE AUTHOR.

Edited and designed by Nia Jones

Printed in the United States of America

89 90 91 92 93 94 / LP / 10 9 8 7 6 5 4 3 2 1

Other books by Andre Bustanoby:

Being a Single Parent
Being a Success at Who You Are: Personalities that Win
But I Didn't Want a Divorce
Eight Keys to Communicate Better
Just Friends
The Readymade Family: How to Be a Stepparent and
  Survive
Just Talk To Me: Talking and Listening for a Happier
  Marriage
  (Andre Bustanoby, with Fay Bustanoby)

CONTENTS

INTRODUCTION

Last year, the marital knot was tied about two million times in the United States. That rate has remained fairly consistent over the past few years; however, it appears that "mixed" marriages are becoming more and more common. Although no reliable figures are available, recently 21 percent of the Catholics surveyed were in mixed marriages and 11 percent of the Protestants.[1] Feeling less bound by the authority of their church, Catholics now seem more willing than ever to marry non-Catholics, and among Protestants, marriages between Christians and non-Christians are increasing.

There are two reasons for these mixed marriages. First, Christians don't seem to feel as negatively about these marriages as they once did. Though mixed marriages still are not generally approved by evangelicals, they are not stigmatized as they once were. Secondly, many couples are marrying later in life. Forty-one percent of single Protestants surveyed and 57 percent of single Catholics under thirty have never married.[2] Young women who hear their biological clocks ticking feel pressured because they are conscious that their childbearing years are slipping away. As a result, more and more Christian women are choosing to marry men who do not profess Christ as Savior.

For Christian men, the motivation to marry an unbeliever is different. When Christian men marry non-Christian women, it's usually not due to the unavailability of

Christian women. Though Christian women are available, men often place a higher priority on the women's looks, personality, or station in life. However when Christian men choose to marry non-Christian women, their marriages may prove disappointing in later years, particularly if their own growing spiritual interests are not shared.

Not all Christians married to unbelievers are in mixed marriages by choice. Some honestly believed they were marrying Christians; others were not believers themselves when they married. Although Christians who were not Christians when they married may attribute marital unhappiness to the fact that their mates are not Christians, they usually do not experience the regret of the ones who knowingly married unbelievers.

Allow me to clarify: My book does *not* endorse or sanction a believer marrying an unbeliever. Such a union can be a serious source of conflict, as you will see in the example of Moses. The believer is opening himself or herself to untold spiritual and emotional problems because of the vast difference that exists between a believer and an unbeliever. Romans 14:23, which says, "Everything that does not come from faith is sin," is referring particularly to Christian liberty. The person in question is *permitted to eat and drink* as long as he does not condemn himself for allowing this liberty. It is in the *self*-condemnation that he sins, since he does not have the faith to believe that it's okay to eat and drink.

Likewise in 1 Corinthians 8:7, it is the individual's conscience that is an issue here, not sinning against God. Of course, if we don't handle our liberty wisely, we may cause ourselves or others to stumble. Then the sin is our failure to handle our liberty wisely, not what we actually do.

Although the counseling sessions I refer to in this book deal with a Christian woman's marriage to an unbeliever, Christian men married to non-Christian women must understand I hold out hope for them, too. The purpose of my book is to help already married believers come to terms with their present condition and recognize that *there is hope* even though they might now be in very unhappy situations. God remains God when we turn to Him in any circumstance of life.

1

Is Marriage to an Unbeliever without Hope?

Cindy heard the biological clock ticking. She had come to me for counsel because her marriage to Bobby, an unbeliever, was deteriorating rapidly.

Cindy became a Christian when she was fifteen and was thoroughly sold on the idea that Christians shouldn't marry non-Christians. When she was in high school, she wouldn't even date a boy if he were not a Christian. "The kind of people you date are the kind of people you marry," she would tell her friends.

In spite of this conviction, she kept running into a problem that seemed to have no solution. There were not enough nice Christian guys to go around. And someone else always seemed to get the Christian athletes or class presidents.

Her situation at State University was even more grim. Christian men simply were not to be found. Belonging to a Christian campus organization didn't seem to improve her chances of meeting Mr. Christian Wonderful either. "You wouldn't believe how many really weird guys were in that group," she said. "They were either uptight Bible-thumpers or wimps. Even the attractive guys turned me

off. They were super-egotistical or users—they knew
there were plenty of Christian girls around and would
date one until they got tired of her and then move on to
the next."

Cindy became quiet and thoughtful. "I guess this is
when I became cynical and drifted from the Lord. It
wasn't obvious at first. I still went to Bible studies and
church. I went through all the rituals, but something
happened inside me. I felt that God didn't really love me.
He knew my need for a decent husband, but He just
didn't come through. So I decided to do it on my own.

"I started to notice the non-Christian guys on campus.
I hung around with them and sent them the message that
I was available to date. You know what I mean—a
woman can tell a man what she has on her mind just by
the way she looks at him and behaves around him. I'm
not talking about anything immoral—just that I wanted
to get to know them better.

"Finally, my girlfriend's boyfriend had a roommate
who wanted to meet me. His name was Robert. He didn't
go by the usual nickname, Bob. He preferred Bobby. I
didn't think anything about it at the time, even though
Bobby is the diminutive form of the name, and more
boyish than the nickname Bob or the given name of
Robert. I guess I didn't think anything about it because he
was good-looking and very personable. He was not a
wimp but a really nice guy, and tremendously thoughtful.
He made me feel like a princess.

"I was pretty sure Bobby wasn't a born-again Christian," Cindy continued, "just by the way he talked.
Nothing vulgar or obscene, you understand. But he
didn't use the usual Christian cliches, and his conversation didn't revolve around the Bible, church, or Bible
studies. Funny thing about that, it actually felt good to be
talking about something different for a change."

Cindy begun to feel stifled and inhibited around

Christians. She told me, "I felt stifled because it seemed that the only things my Christian friends ever talked about were the Bible and Christianity. It seemed that any other subject was 'unspiritual.' I felt inhibited because it seemed that my friends were always watching to see if I lived up to the name 'Christian.' That's okay. I know we ought to watch out for each other. But it seemed that the motive was to catch someone in sin so we could have something to gossip about. Of course, Christians never gossip, so we just 'shared our concerns so we could pray' for our friends."

Cindy became quiet and thoughtful again. "I *do* sound cynical, don't I?" She shrugged her shoulders and continued with her story.

"Bobby and I went together for about two years. He graduated and went on to law school. I was a year behind him, and when I graduated, we married. The plan was for me to work and help him through the rest of law school.

"He did very well in school, and when he graduated he landed a great job with a law firm practicing corporate law. He always laughed and said that he didn't have the stomach to practice criminal law. I didn't think much of that remark, even though he said it a number of times over the years. In fact, it took me thirteen years to put the picture together—to understand how I could be so desperately unhappy with this *nice* guy.

"Please understand that I'm not being cynical when I call him a nice guy. He really is, and all my friends, even my Christian friends, tell me what a wonderful husband I have. In fact, in many ways he is closer to the Christian ideal than a lot of the Christian husbands my girlfriends are married to. He's a wonderful father. He supports me well and doesn't complain about my spending habits. In fact, he doesn't complain about *anything!* Of course, nice guys don't complain—that wouldn't be nice."

Cindy interrupted her train of thought to explain

something. Mentioning "nice guy" triggered a thought she didn't want to forget.

"By the way, I finally figured out why Robert prefers to be called Bobby. The diminutive form of the name really suits his nice-guy image. Robert _____ III sounds very formidable. But a Bobby wouldn't hurt a fly. When I told him why I thought he liked to be called Bobby, he said I was right. But then I asked him why on earth he chose a profession like law that is so adversarial. He just laughed and said, 'Yes, it's adversarial, but it's all ritualized and follows very strict rules of procedure. It's like knights jousting, and the best man wins. But there's nothing personal about it. Outside the courtroom I'm the best of friends with my colleagues.'"

Cindy again became quiet and thoughtful. Finally she spoke.

"It was after this conversation that I began to put things together—why I feel as I do about Bobby. Would it sound strange if I told you that I think it's possible to be too much of a nice guy? I don't mean that Bobby's phony. He really is nice. But he's *too* nice. What I mean is that he's the original hear-no-evil, see-no-evil, speak-no-evil. He seems incapable of seeing hostile intent in anyone. This is why I think he's so good in court and such an excellent attorney. He absolutely cannot be rattled, and he uses such finesse in the way he handles people."

Cindy then looked at me wide-eyed and demanded, "Do you think I'm crazy?"

Before I could answer she said, "My friends think I'm crazy. But let me tell you why I feel as I do. Bobby is a man of principle and conviction. But because he is so concerned about making everyone happy and sugarcoating everything, I'm afraid the day will come when he will have to choose between confronting a person or giving up a principle and that he'll give up his principle rather than confront.

"We had a very heated conversation the other night—no, I had a very heated conversation. Bobby doesn't get heated. He smiles when he talks. I told him that I didn't understand how he, the super nice guy, could practice such an uncompromising profession as law. The law is law. It is very clear and very rigid.

"Again, he laughed—he *always* smiles and laughs. He said, 'It's not that clear. There are many ambiguities. Nor is it rigid. When the law doesn't serve us any longer, legislators change it. Even the Constitution can be amended.'

"Then he became serious. He said something he had never said before. He told me the trouble with Christians is that they're always looking for someone to condemn and send to hell. He wanted to know if I really believed that people deserve that kind of fate.

"I couldn't believe what I was hearing. This nice guy couldn't stand to have *anyone* unhappy. To him, not even the worst sinner deserved hell. At that moment a fantasy flashed through my mind. My fantasy was of a burglar who breaks into our home at night, grabs me and starts to rape me while Bobby stands by and says, 'You really shouldn't do that. Can't we talk?'

"When I told Bobby what I was thinking, he didn't get mad. He just turned to stone. I know that I hurt his feelings; he didn't talk to me for the rest of the evening.

"The next day I told him that I was sorry I hurt his feelings. But his response left me without any hope that we would ever see eye to eye on anything. He told me, 'Cindy, this is one reason why I'm not a Christian. All of you Christians are a violent, bloody bunch of people. Your own Bible speaks in praise of the violent invasion of Canaan and the murder of innocent women and children. And you couldn't have a bloodless salvation. Your Jesus had to shed blood—crucified at that!' "

For a long time Cindy sat in silence. Finally she said,

"You know the uptight Bible-thumpers I once despised? They don't look so bad now. Yes, sometimes they overdo it and alienate people with their aggressiveness. But a little of that aggressiveness in Bobby would make me feel a lot more secure."

Another pause, and then, "We have another problem now that worries me more. Even though Bobby permits me to take the kids to a Bible-teaching church, he undercuts their faith in subtle ways.

"For example, when their Sunday school lesson was on creation versus evolution, we talked about it at home, and Bobby took the evolutionist's side. He wasn't pushy about it. He just said that he wanted the kids to understand that there was another point of view besides creation.

"Bobby does this a lot. He is always taking issue with what is taught in Sunday school or church. He's never nasty about it. But it continually raises a barrier between us.

"I pray for Bobby's salvation. But I feel selfish when I do. I want him to be a Christian because it would make my life happier, and it would relieve me of my guilt over marrying a non-Christian. I think that the problems we are having in our marriage are due to the fact that I sinned in marrying Bobby—you know, the unequal yoke. What can I do?"

■　■　■

Indeed, what *can* she do? There are no easy solutions. Like many others with similar questions, Cindy needed some fresh insight into her situation, both psychologically and theologically.

Psychologically, the marriage would need help even if Bobby became a Christian. He had a neurotic commitment to a nice guy facade that arose from an overly conventional personality.[1] Bobby would still have a great deal of trouble dealing with anything that remotely resembled disagreement or hostility. He would always leave Cindy with the feeling that her welfare might be compromised if he had to fight for a principle.

Theologically speaking, Bobby would continue to have difficulty understanding why Cindy was bothered about people who didn't bother him at all. As a non-Christian, Bobby was able to make Cindy feel that, as a Christian, she should be more tolerant of people. Even if Bobby became a Christian, there was a danger that he might become even more neurotically committed to his overly conventional way of handling things and make Cindy feel increasingly guilty for her seeming intolerance.

It's very important for Christians married to unbelievers to recognize that unhappiness and conflict in marriage may not be due to the fact that the mate is an unbeliever. Conflict often continues even after the mate becomes a Christian.

Cindy was convinced, however, that the root of her problem was sin. She believed she had sinned by marrying an unbeliever and now, as a result, was unequally yoked. As long as she was unequally yoked, she would never be happy. Cindy needed to see that the Bible is not quite as gloomy about mixed marriages as she. She needed some fresh insight into the issue of the unequal yoke.

2

What Is the "Unequal Yoke"?

Whenever mixed marriages are discussed, the question of the unequal yoke is certain to be raised. It is a matter of concern both to the person who becomes a Christian after marriage and to the Christian who marries a non-Christian, whether in ignorance or by choice. At issue is the apostle Paul's warning in 2 Corinthians 6:14–7:1:

> Do not be yoked together with unbelievers. For what do righteousness and wickedness have in common? Or what fellowship can light have with darkness? What harmony is there between Christ and Belial? What does a believer have in common with an unbeliever? What agreement is there between the temple of God and idols? For we are the temple of the living God. As God has said: "I will live with them and walk among them, and I will be their God, and they will be my people."
>
> "Therefore come out from them and be separate, says the Lord. Touch no unclean thing, and I will receive you.
>
> "I will be a Father to you, and you will be my sons and daughters, says the Lord Almighty." Since we have these promises, dear friends, let us purify our-

selves from everything that contaminates body and spirit, perfecting holiness out of reverence for God.

This Scripture refers to a number of Old Testament passages about Israel's return from the Babylonian captivity. Because of her idolatry, Israel was carried off captive to Babylon in the seventh and sixth centuries B.C. The Israelites, prior to their captivity, didn't merely associate with, or live "in" the world of, the idolaters; they became idolaters, too. The Babylonian captivity was God's way of saying, "If you're going to behave as pigs, maybe a stint in the pigpen will cure you." Allow me to explain that I don't use the words *pig* and *pigpen* to insult Gentiles. The meaning is suggested by the language Paul uses in 2 Corinthians 7:1, where he says that we are to *purify* ourselves. The ancient Greeks used the word *purify* to describe the kind of cleansing a person needs when he's been in a pigpen. God's discipline for Israel worked. The pigpen of Babylon, where some of the worst forms of idolatry were practiced, was so awful to the Jews that they were cured of idolatry.

If we are to understand the unequal yoke of 2 Corinthians 6, it's important that we understand the historical parallel. Israel was guilty of far more than merely associating with unbelievers by marrying them or conducting business with them. They actually had slipped into imitating their idolatrous ways in their personal and professional lives.

Centuries later, the Corinthian Christians found themselves in a similar situation. In Corinth, some of the worst forms of idolatry were practiced. The priestesses in the heathen temples actually were prostitutes. Idolaters who engaged in sexual intercourse with them were considered to be performing *acts of worship* to the gods of fertility. In Paul's first letter to the Corinthians, he warned them about eating meat that came from an idolatrous sacrifice (1 Cor. 8:1–11). Though under certain circumstances, the

Corinthians were permitted to eat this meat and even to eat a sacrificial meal with unbelievers, they were warned that this kind of compromise could lead to something far worse; namely, resumption of the idolatrous habits they practiced before coming to Christ.

By the time Paul wrote his second letter to the Corinthians, his worst fears had been realized. The Corinthian Christians were not merely associating with the unbelievers; they were now in the pigpen, in the same position as Israel during the Babylonian captivity. They had become so idolatrous in their behavior that God let them be swallowed up by the pagan culture.

To define the "unequal yoke," we must realize it is not something as innocuous as being married to an unbeliever or being in a business partnership with an unbeliever, nor eating meat from an idolatrous sacrifice with unbelievers, a practice that was permitted under some circumstances (1 Cor. 8:1–11:1). The command to come out and be separate is a command to come out of the Babylonian captivity in body and spirit (2 Cor. 7:1). For us to interpret the "unequal yoke" as merely marriage to an unbeliever misses the seriousness of the situation. To be unequally yoked with an unbeliever is to be bound in any relationship, whether in marriage, in business, or in whatever circumstances, with an unrestrained practicing idolater, one who openly and emphatically rejects God, and to participate with him in his ungodly behavior.

Paul asks, "What harmony is there between Christ and Belial?" (2 Cor. 6:15). Belial is a name for Satan, and this is the only time it is used in the New Testament. Coming from two Hebrew words meaning "without yoke," it refers to unrestrained, unyoked licentiousness. Satan is so named because he is the father of unrestrained idolatrous behavior, such as the Corinthians display.

Paul says, "Don't yoke yourselves with the unyoked ones—those who are unrestrained." The problem is not that the Corinthian Christians were merely eating with unbelievers or even marrying them. They had actually *joined with* idolaters, indulging in the worst forms of sin imaginable, just as they had before they knew Christ. If we interpret marriage to an unbeliever as an example of the unequal yoke, we miss the seriousness of Paul's warning.

Paul's warning is much the same as the one given in Proverbs 1:10, 11, where we are warned about unbelievers who are totally unrestrained and told not to cast our lot with them. But are all unbelievers so bad? Some unbelievers seem to be okay people—nice enough. True, all unbelievers are not unrestrained in their actions. We must, therefore, make a distinction between *restrained* and *unrestrained* unbelievers.

We make this distinction naturally when we consider other forms of yoking. Business partnerships are a good example. They are as legally binding, as fraught with emotion, and as involved with values and ideals as marriage relationships, but Christians do not automatically avoid the yoke of a business partnership just because the other person is not a believer. Rather, business partnerships are decided on the basis of the partner's competence and business ethics, though it would be nice for the partner to be a Christian, too. But having a partner who is a Christian is no substitute for his not being competent or ethical. Sadly, the person who says he is a Christian is not always ethical.

Participation in non-Christian professional organizations must be decided on the same basis. Does the professional organization have an ethical code of practice and enforce it in its membership? We must evaluate carefully how such organizations do business and handle their memberships.

Now we see that the warning about the unequal yoke is not a warning against mere associations with unbelievers, whether in marriage, business, or professional organizations. It is a warning against joining the children of Belial, the unrestrained ones, and behaving as they do. It is a warning against *union of any kind* with practicing idolaters who show their devotion to Satan through unrestrained licentiousness.

VALUES AND RESTRAINED UNBELIEVERS

One of the major problems in Corinth both for the unbelievers and the believers was lack of sexual restraint. Many of the Corinthian unbelievers plunged into their worship of Aphrodite without restraint, visiting the temple prostitutes on a regular basis. Evidently, some Christians at Corinth became involved in a life of sexual permissiveness, too, because of their close association or "yoke" with these unrestrained unbelievers. The yoking probably included both marriage and business partnerships. This close association led them to adopt a life of unrestraint, a life that included sexual permissiveness, sometimes to a greater degree than the pagans. At least one Corinthian Christian committed fornication with his father's wife, which was probably his stepmother (1 Cor. 5:1).

Not all Greeks were unrestrained unbelievers. Some were very moral, as Paul points out in his letter to the Romans:

> Indeed, when Gentiles, who do not have the (Mosaic) law, do by nature things required by the law, they are a law for themselves, even though they do not have the (Mosaic) law, since they show that the requirements of the law are written on their hearts, their consciences also bearing witness. . . ." (Rom. 2:14–15).

Unbelieving people, though fallen, still have a conscience that tells them where they must practice restraint. Though following their conscience did not save them, many Greeks lived lives that put to shame the Christians in the Corinthian church. Though the yoke of marriage or a business partnership with a "restrained" unbeliever might not be a wise move, unbelievers who are sensitive to a God-given conscience are more compatible with believers than most of us like to admit.

Restrained unbelievers often restrain themselves from being as bad as they can be because they find that they are happier and healthier if they practice restraint. In their personal lives they are faithful to one wife, and in their business dealings they are honest and can be trusted.

Though some restrained unbelievers mistakenly believe that their goodness will lead to salvation, the *practical* value of their good behavior should not be ignored or discounted. It enables us to work together with them in maintaining homes and a society that are well ordered and promote the well-being of society.

We need to remember that our cooperation with unbelievers having like values will not usher in the millennium. Only Jesus' return to the earth will do that. But God has not yet turned the world over to Satan. He still is working through the Holy Spirit in the hearts of unbelievers to restrain evil and promote good—a work designed to make the world livable until Jesus comes again.

Though the believer has nothing in common with the unbeliever in his understanding of *spiritual things*, we still can cooperate to our mutual benefit on the things we *do* understand and value—how to live a successful life on earth. The Christian married to a "restrained" unbeliever who has similar values because of his God-given conscience would do well to promote those values they hold in common. In the Appendix, I have provided a "Values Exercise" that can be used by the Christian and non-Christian husband and wife to identify the values they agree on and promote cooperation in the pursuit of those values.

MOSES MARRIED AN UNBELIEVER

This view, with its distinction between unbelievers and practicing idolaters, is consistent with the Old Testament teaching about marriage. The Mosaic Law did not forbid marriages between the Israelites and the heathen nations, with the exception of those tribes living in Canaan (Exod. 34:15–16; Deut. 7:1–3).[1]

In Exodus 34:15, "those who live in the land" are the Canaanites and six other tribes listed in Deuteronomy 7:1. But by the time of Ezra, three more groups were added to the forbidden list: the Ammonites, Moabites, and Egyptians (Ezra 9:1–2). Why are the Egyptians included by Ezra when, at the time of Moses, they were not?

Ezra wanted to be sure that the people who returned to Canaan from the Babylonian captivity did not relapse into idolatry. By now, depopulated Canaan had been occupied by the Ammonites, Moabites, and Egyptians and had become corrupted by the Canaanites. For this reason, even the Egyptians in Canaan were no longer suitable marriage partners.

But it was not always so. The tribes that God warns Moses about in Exodus 34 were not merely unbelievers but were idolaters of the worst sort. For this reason, the Jews at one time could marry Egyptians, but not anyone from the tribes of Canaan.[2]

Ezra's concern is the same as Paul's. They were not dealing with mere unbelievers. They were dealing with the children of Belial—the unrestrained ones, idolaters. Distinguishing between mere unbelievers and the children of Belial is the key to understanding what the unequal yoke is. When taken in the context of Corinth's idolatry, Paul is talking about *unrestrained* unbelievers. Malachi also distinguished between them when he lamented,

"Judah has desecrated the sanctuary the LORD loves,
by marrying the daughter of a foreign god" (Mal. 2:11).

The expression, "daughter of a foreign god," refers to
heathen women who refused to give up their idolatry.[3]
They must be distinguished from those who did not
practice idolatry but still were unbelievers. Marriage to
practicing idolators was forbidden. Marriage to mere
unbelievers, though unwise, was not expressly forbidden.

I am not encouraging believers to marry unbelievers.
There are good reasons for not marrying an unbeliever;
however, there is a difference between conscious sinning
and acting unwisely.

The marriage of Moses tells us a great deal about the
marriage of believers and unbelievers in Old Testament
times. After murdering the Egyptian slave master, Moses
fled to Midian where he met Zipporah, the daughter of
Reuel (Exod. 2 and 3). *Reuel* means "friend of God." Even
though he was a Midianite, Reuel (also known as Jethro)
was a priest of Israel's God. He probably was a believer in
the Old Testament sense. But the same cannot be inferred
about Zipporah, his daughter, whom Moses married.

It was at this time that Moses encountered God at the
burning bush and was commissioned to go back to Egypt
and rescue God's people. On the return trip to Egypt,
Zipporah's unbelief is revealed (Exod. 4:18–26).

The telling incident occurred when it came time to
circumcise Moses' second son. To the Jews, circumcision
was a sacred sign of God's covenant with them, a
reminder that they truly were His chosen people (Gen.
17:1–10). But Moses had neglected to circumcise his
youngest son, most likely to appease Zipporah, who
thought the ritual disgusting.

While Moses was on his way back to Egypt with
Zipporah and his two sons, God threatened him with
death for failing to circumcise his son. Evidently, God

inflicted Moses with some sickness that incapacitated him because he could not circumcise the boy immediately. Zipporah had to do it. This forced her to show her true colors. We are told,

> Zipporah took a flint knife, cut off her son's foreskin and touched Moses' feet with it (literally, threw it at his feet). "Surely you are a bridegroom of blood to me," she said. So the LORD let him alone (Exod. 4:25–26).

Zipporah really threw a tantrum! She called Moses a "bridegroom of blood" because the only way she could rescue her husband from the jaws of death, the only way she could save her husband's life, was by circumcising her son. That meant blood would be shed. And this was distasteful to her.

If we read between the lines, we can surmise that Zipporah threw such a fit after the circumcision of their first son that Moses simply did not circumcise his second son. Zipporah was much like Bobby in chapter 1. A bloody religion is terribly distasteful to unbelievers.

Though Moses was God's chosen instrument to lead His people out of Egypt, Zipporah's unbelief was a terrible impediment to Moses. But he did not divorce her. We are told that he sent her and their two sons back to her father (Exod. 18:2).

By now it was clear to Moses that, though his wife was not a practicing idolater, she still was an unbeliever who had a keen distaste for the bloody religion of the Jews. She would never understand her husband's mission to redeem God's people from Egypt. And we may conclude that she would have opposed the sacrifice of the Passover lamb that would save Israel's firstborn sons.

We cannot be certain how long Moses and Zipporah were separated. It may have taken up to a year for Moses to gain Israel's freedom and lead them as far as Sinai, where he was reunited with Zipporah (Exod. 18:5–6). I say reunited and not reconciled because there is no mention that Zipporah had become a believer or had even apologized for her behavior. In fact, this is the last we hear about Zipporah. Her death is not even recorded. We may assume that she and Moses continued to live together as husband and wife, but there is no record of any more children by this union.

The important lesson we learn from Moses and Zipporah is that God did permit His chosen leader to marry an unbeliever, but the union made Moses' work more difficult. If, as the apostle Paul points out, marriage itself distracts us from God's work, then marriage to an unbeliever would be even more distracting (1 Cor. 7:32–35). But marriage to unbelievers was not forbidden in the Old Testament, nor is it today.

HOSEA MARRIED THE DAUGHTER OF FRUITCAKES

One of the strangest marriages in the Bible is the marriage of the prophet Hosea. He was *commanded* by God to marry a harlot and raise the children born of her illicit relationships as his own children (Hos. 1:2).

Hosea married Gomer, daughter of Diblaim (Hos. 1:3). The word *diblaim* means "fruitcakes" and refers to raisins or figs pressed together in cakes and offered to heathen deities.[4] This name tells us something of Gomer's background. This daughter of "fruitcakes" apparently was the child of idolatrous parents. Yet, because Israelites were forbidden to marry practicing idolaters, it's unlikely that Gomer practiced idolatry. But she was influenced by the immorality of the system, for she was a harlot, and her behavior shows that she was not a true believer.

If marriage to an unbeliever had been forbidden by God, He never would have instructed Hosea to marry Gomer. Though such marriages may interfere with the believer's service to God, as we saw in the case of Moses, the union of the believer and unbeliever is not a sin.

WHAT IS THE "UNEQUAL YOKE"?

What, then, should we make of Paul's command in 2 Corinthians about the unequal yoke? The warning is a command to stop joining the practicing idolaters in their unrestrained pursuit of idolatry. Sometimes eating with these people had even degenerated into behaving like them. They had not heeded Paul's warnings in his first letter (1 Cor. 8:1–11:1). As a result of carelessness, they had slipped back into idolatry.

This interpretation is validated by the larger context. Paul has been urging them to take seriously the fact that they had a ministry of reconciliation committed to them (2 Cor. 5:11–6:10). They could not possibly perform this ministry as long as they were living in "Babylonian captivity." They, like Israel, had to come out of the Babylonian captivity of body and spirit.

To summarize, in view of the Corinthians' idolatry, marriage to mere unbelievers is not the issue, nor is it serious enough to constitute an unequal yoke. Furthermore, the Old Testament makes it clear that associations with unbelievers, even *marriage* to them, were permitted as long as they were not actively engaged in idolatry. The most compelling argument supporting this viewpoint is found in 1 Corinthians 7:12–14, where Scripture teaches that marriage between a believer and unbeliever actually brings the unbeliever into a new relationship with God.

3

Is Sanctification Contagious?

"Do you believe that all non-Christians are doomed to hell?" Bobby, Cindy's husband, was uncharacteristically blunt. When he asked me this question, he didn't sound like the nice guy that Cindy had described on her previous visit.

I had asked Cindy to bring Bobby with her when she saw me again. As he sat in my office, he appeared relaxed, but he wanted an answer.

"If you are asking me if I believe that all people without Christ are unsaved, I must say yes. If, on the other hand, you are asking if I believe that non-Christians cannot be good people or do good things, I must say no, I don't believe that. In fact, the Bible says that because you married a Christian woman, you are sanctified—you have been set apart from the rest of unbelieving humanity to be used by God. Bobby, you are a special person."

Bobby probably thought that I was trying to butter him up because he just smiled and said, "Okay, if you say so." He then went on to challenge the Christian belief that people without Christ are unsaved.

"I don't think it's going to be profitable for us to argue that point," I said. "The important thing is that your marriage is in trouble, and Cindy feels that the reason for the trouble is that she has sinned. She believes that she disobeyed God when she married you, because you are not a believer. She thinks that God can't bless her marriage because of her disobedience."

Cindy had explained her problem to Bobby, so he understood what I was talking about. But to him this was just another example of Christian bigotry, which now was threatening his marriage.

Before Bobby could derail me again I said, "I don't think that either you or Cindy appreciate what you have in your marriage. When I told you that your marriage to Cindy made you a special person in God's eyes, I wasn't trying to patronize you. Let me share with both of you the Christian view of mixed marriage."

> If any brother has a wife who is not a believer and she is willing to live with him, he must not divorce her. And if a woman has a husband who is not a believer and he is willing to live with her, she must not divorce him. For the unbelieving husband has been sanctified through his wife, and the unbelieving wife has been sanctified through her believing husband. Otherwise your children would be unclean, but as it is, they are holy (1 Cor. 7:12–14).

■ ■ ■

WHAT IS SANCTIFICATION?

The word "sanctity" means "holy." In the Bible, both persons and things are declared to be holy. In this case, the holiness has nothing to do with the behavior of the person. It has to do with his or her unique position—set apart for God's use—as opposed to that which is common and suited to everyday use.

The opposite of sanctified is *unclean* (1 Cor. 7:14). Unclean does not have to do with the morality of the person. It means that he is common, not set apart for God's service. Both the unbelieving mate and children are sanctified by their relationship with the Christian mate and parent.

Evidently, the children are mentioned because the Corinthians had already accepted the teaching that unbelieving children have a special relationship with God since they have been born of a believing parent. Paul now makes it clear that the unbelieving mate enjoys the same privilege through marriage. The Christian mate and parent in a family is a contagious person, infecting both mate and children with sanctification!

But what is this condition they are "infected" with? What does it mean to be "set apart for God"? The common interpretation is that this sanctification puts the unbeliever in a special position where he has the advantage of a continual exposure to the gospel in a way that other people do not have. Although this may be a true statement of what happens to the sanctified unbeliever, this interpretation does not do justice to the word "sanctity," which has to do with the usability of the person or object sanctified. That which is sanctified is not only set apart to receive something from God but is also to be used by God.

Bobby was truly being used by God. As a sanctified unbeliever, he was a blessing to Cindy and to the church, but she could not acknowledge it nor could she see it. Bobby was an unbeliever, and she could not see unbelievers doing anything good.

Though Bobby was not a Christian, and even though

he objected to his wife's bloody religion, he was a very gracious and giving person. He and Cindy had a lovely home, and he was quite willing to let her use it for women's Bible studies and after-church fellowships. Though he did not attend church, he always assisted Cindy when they hosted church functions in their home. As a good host, he never raised controversial issues with his guests, even though he felt that many Christians were narrow-minded.

Bobby also was generous with his money. He didn't object to Cindy's tithing, though he did insist on designating it to causes that he considered worthy, such as famine relief.

He was a good father and was interested in becoming active in some program that would develop the moral, physical, social, and intellectual skills of boys. He owned a large sailboat and was an excellent seaman. I was not surprised when he approached Cindy with the idea of beginning a Sea Scout or Explorer Scout Troop in the church and using his boat to teach the boys seamanship.

When Cindy asked me what I thought, I replied that I thought it was an excellent idea and suggested that they approach Cindy's pastor. Even though he knew that Bobby was not a Christian, their pastor saw this idea as an excellent opportunity, not only for Bobby to serve God as a "sanctified unbeliever," but also for the men of the church to have an opportunity to work with Bobby in the troop and witness to him.

Unfortunately, the Christian education committee turned down the idea. They argued that only Christian men should lead the boys in the church. And furthermore, the Explorer and Sea Scout programs were not "spiritual." If they were going to have a program for boys in the church, it would be a Christian program.

I felt sad that the church was missing such an excellent opportunity. Obviously, their idea of sanctification was more limited than mine, and they had difficulty understanding the unique position that Bobby enjoys as the husband of a Christian wife. Exposure to Christian men working and sailing together would have been a natural way to keep the gospel before him.

As the apostle Paul said, "How do you know, wife, whether you will save your husband? Or, how do you know, husband, whether you will save your wife?" (1 Cor. 7:16). Someone may say, "Doesn't this verse support the usual interpretation of this passage—that sanctification merely places a person in a position where he is exposed to the gospel and nothing more?" No, it does not. Being in a position where he can be exposed to the gospel is only a secondary benefit. Cindy's church kept Bobby at arm's length by not making him a part of their program, by not letting him get close enough for effective personal contact. We must see unbelievers in a unique way if we are to be effective witnesses to them.

CINDY'S BREAKTHROUGH

This incident made Cindy reconsider her attitude toward unbelievers in general and Bobby in particular. Though Bobby took the decision of the church calmly, Cindy was furious.

"After all Bobby has done for this church, they treat him as a leper. He has opened our home to them, he has given his money, he has even made repairs on the church building and purchased equipment for them at cost and installed it. And *this* is the way they treat him! He's not asking for a position of spiritual leadership in the church. He wants to teach boys *seamanship!* Do *Christian* seamen handle sails and ropes differently than *non-Christian* seamen?''

I pointed out to Cindy that though it is true there is a unique Christian approach to everything we do in life, even seamanship, she was asking an important question. Do non-Christians have anything to teach Christians? Obviously, the answer is yes. The fact that unbelievers have made the greatest advances in man's understanding of how God's world functions is proof enough. Non-Christians *have a great deal* to teach Christians.

Cindy began to see that her view of how God worked in His world had been very narrow. Until now, she thought of God's work only in terms of His saving work, and she divided all of humanity into two classes: Christian and non-Christian. She saw all non-Christians in terms of their spiritual state—lost. To acknowledge that they could do anything good seemed to her to minimize their fallen condition and their need to be saved.

The idea that God should be doing anything else in the world besides saving people simply hadn't occurred to her. She knew vaguely that it was God's work to keep the world functioning. People needed to be fed and healed; criminals needed to be brought to justice. But all of that seemed incidental and remote from God's work of saving people's souls. The idea that God is actively at work in unbelievers, particularly men like Bobby who are sanctified to special service for God, was something new.

This new insight began to have an effect on Cindy's marriage. She began to see Bobby in a different light. Though he was lost, she saw God at work in his life, and she began to appreciate the fact that Bobby's good deeds *were a work of God.* Cindy began to let Bobby know that she appreciated him and all that he had done for her and the children, and for her church.

She also stopped a bad habit she had developed. Because she wanted Bobby to understand that he could not be saved by his own works but only by Jesus Christ, she had continually put down the good things that he did. In one way or another she had given Bobby the message, "The good things you do are nice, but I really can't get excited over them because, after all, your good work won't get you to heaven."

This attitude always had made Bobby furious. Cindy couldn't appreciate the things he had done as things good in, of, and by themselves. She always connected them with a "works" type of salvation, which the Bible clearly denounces, even though this was not why Bobby did the good things he did. When Cindy began to appreciate what Bobby was doing as a father, community leader, and attorney, Bobby's attitude toward her began to change. Feeling appreciated by her, he began to show his appreciation for her.

AN OPPORTUNITY FOR WITNESS

Cindy was still troubled, so she asked to see me privately.

"How do you witness to a man like Bobby? I understand now that I've been wrong to beat him over the head with the fact that he's a sinner and that he can't buy his way into heaven with good works. But I'm afraid that if I don't remind him of these things, he'll think he's going to heaven because of his good works. I'm afraid that he'll get smug and self-satisfied now that I'm building him up."

I pointed out to Cindy that the answer to witnessing to a man like this is not to denigrate his good works. Rather, we are to praise what is good, but we do it with the attitude that it is *God's* working through the unbeliever that makes it praiseworthy. I opened my Bible to Psalm 19:1 and began reading. "The heavens declare the glory of God; the skies proclaim the work of his hands."

After reading the first four verses I said, "Creation speaks and pours out knowledge in every tongue known to man. The apostle Paul goes so far as to say that we can learn from nature (1 Cor. 11:14). All truth is God's truth, whether it is revealed in nature or in the Bible. And we should look for harmony in the truth that comes from both sources.

Cindy was uneasy about this. The idea that God should speak through any other source than the Bible was foreign to her. Yet she had to acknowledge that the message of the psalm is clear. God does speak through nature.

"But where do you get the idea that the unbeliever hears and responds to God's revelation of Himself in nature?" Cindy asked.

"Look at Romans 1:18–20," I replied.

> The wrath of God is being revealed from heaven against all the godlessness and wickedness of men who suppress the truth by their wickedness, since what may be known about God is plain to them, because God has made it plain to them. For since the creation of the world God's invisible qualities—his eternal power and divine nature—have been clearly seen, being understood from what has been made, so that men are without excuse.

THE SIN OF INGRATITUDE

I explained to Cindy, "God is speaking through His creation and is saying to Bobby, 'I am your Creator, and you owe your worship to Me.' People like Bobby need to know that God *is* speaking to them and that God has a claim on them.

"The problem with unbelievers like Bobby is not ignorance. Their problem is ingratitude for all the good things God gives them."

I continued to read Romans 1:21, 22.

> For although they knew God, they neither glorified him as God nor gave thanks to him, but their thinking became futile and their foolish hearts were darkened. Although they claimed to be wise, they became fools and exchanged the glory of the immortal God for images made to look like mortal man. . . .

I explained to Cindy that God shows the unbeliever that He is the source of every good gift to the human race, but the unbeliever responds by denying God's existence and giving himself the credit for the good things the human race enjoys.

"Cindy, I have a great deal of good to say about unbelievers and their ability to do marvelous things. Though we have suffered destructive wars, and though crime is a serious problem people are able to control these evil passions well enough to survive. And they are able to do these things even though they are fallen and in rebellion against God."

I then drew this analogy.

"Let's look at it this way. A ship embarks on a journey, and shortly after it heads out to sea, the crew mutinies against the captain. But they are not able to gain control of the bridge. The captain is able to keep the ship on course. Though the mutineers are in rebellion against the captain, they must keep the ship operating if they are to survive. They must distill fresh water; they must feed themselves; they must even have order and discipline in their ranks to be sure that they don't destroy themselves with total anarchy. They think that they are in charge of their lives and destinies. But the truth is that they are not.

"First, the ship continues on course toward port and a day of reckoning. Second, though they are in rebellion, they must continue to function as responsible seamen if they are to survive.

"The world is like this ship, and God is steering it on His intended course through history toward a day of reckoning. Though unbelievers are in rebellion against Him, they must function responsibly if they are to survive. And they do. Unbelievers have made great advances in science and many other fields because of their abilities as human beings created in God's image. They may not be able to understand the things of the Spirit of God (1 Cor. 2:14), but they are able to understand things pertaining to nature and this world. They are able to understand because God reveals truth, not only through the Bible, but through nature as well.

"Cindy, unbelievers like Bobby are not witnessed to effectively by being told how *bad* they are. I think it is more effective to acknowledge that they are doing a good job of keeping things shipshape, but that they are failing to acknowledge three things: (1) They are doing a good job of keeping planet Earth going because God has taught them how; (2) They are committing the sin of ingratitude by accepting God's gifts but not thanking Him for them; and (3) Though they are in rebellion against God, they still have time to give up and throw themselves on His mercy."

This approach helped Cindy change her attitude toward Bobby. But she still had a long way to go. She was so used to thinking of unbelievers as *bad* and *lost* that it was difficult for her to think of Bobby in positive terms or to see any common ground between them. Cindy needed to remember that though Bobby was lost, he still was a creature made in God's image, accomplishing God's purpose.

4

Blessed Unbeliever:
Image of God?

I was feeling pretty good about Cindy and Bobby. The idea that God was at work in Bobby's life was revolutionary to Cindy and seemed to generate a more positive attitude in both of them. When I saw them again, I was totally unprepared for their change in attitudes.

"You both look depressed," I began. Cindy and Bobby remained silent until the silence became unbearable. Finally Cindy spoke.

"Oh, it's my mother, I told her what you had to say about the sanctification of the unbeliever, and she told me that you're full of hooey."

I had heard of Cindy's mother before in previous conversations. I knew that she was a Christian, but she was also an opinionated woman who tried to run Cindy's life. Now she seemed determined to straighten me out, too, at least indirectly.

"What seems to be your mother's problem?" I asked.

Cindy hesitated. From the way she behaved, I knew that her mother must have had some pretty harsh words for me. Finally she spoke.

"My mother says you're a humanist. She told me that

you don't seem to know that the Bible teaches that the human race is rotten to the core, and she read a bunch of verses from the Bible to prove her point."

From what I could gather, Cindy's mother had read verses such as Ephesians 2:1–3, 1 Corinthians 2:14, and Romans 3:10–18 that portray the human race as spiritually bankrupt—dead in sin, followers of Satan who gratify their sin nature, and the objects of God's wrath. But it was obvious that her mother's understanding of the doctrine of man was seriously limited.

BOBBY, THE IMAGE OF GOD

I needed to know if Cindy's understanding was as limited as her mother's, so I asked, "Cindy, what would you say if I told you that the Bible declares that Bobby is the image of God?"

She looked puzzled, obviously not sure what to think about that statement, so I continued.

"The Bible makes it very clear that even after the fall of the human race, man still was declared to be the image of God. Because he is made in the image of God, we dare not murder another human being (Gen. 9:6), nor do we curse him (James 3:9). God created man in His image to tell us something about what He is like. It's as though a great architect built a beautiful city and then erected an image in it to declare to all the people something about its builder—who and what he is like."

Cindy balked. "How can you say that unbelieving man is the image of God? The Bible makes it clear that the human race is evil to the core. No wonder my mother called you a humanist."

HOW BAD IS THE HUMAN RACE?

Cindy really was backing off by now. Her suspicion of me showed in her eyes, and she needed some biblical assurance that I had not gone off the deep end.

"Your mother is right about the human race when she says it is spiritually bankrupt," I assured her. "Because of this, God had to take the initiative to reconcile the race by sending His son, Jesus, to die for our sins.

"But she is wrong when she talks as though the human race is as bad as it can be. We must make an important distinction here between the spiritual problem and the *metaphysical* problem."

At this point, I lost Cindy. She looked at me blankly and said, "What do you mean by 'spiritual' and 'metaphysical'?"

"Metaphysical has to do with our humanity," I replied. "When man was created, he was created both as a spiritual creature in fellowship with God and as a human creature—the metaphysical side of us—made in the image of God. When Adam sinned and the race fell, spiritually we were cut off from God. No matter how hard the human race may try to reconcile itself to God, it is impossible. In this sense we are spiritually dead and incapable of resurrecting ourselves. This doesn't mean that mankind cannot perform moral acts and behave decently. What it means is that our good behavior has no effect on our relationship with God.

"Though Adam ruined the race spiritually when he sinned, *metaphysically* the situation didn't change. We still were human beings bearing the image of God."

Cindy looked annoyed and impatient. "What does that have to do with anything? You say my mother is right—that the human race is lost without Christ. Isn't that the issue?"

"No," I replied, "it's *not* the issue as far as Bobby is concerned. Bobby's major problem with you, your mother, and most Christians is your *attitude* toward him. Christians don't seem to have anything good to say about unbelievers. You, your mother, and many people in your church make Bobby feel alone and isolated. You build walls around yourselves and then wonder why he acts as though he's an outsider. You don't seem to place any value on the fact that even though the race is fallen, even though Bobby cannot be saved without faith in the finished work of Christ, *he still bears the image of God.*

Cindy finally spoke. "You *do* sound like a humanist. What's so important about valuing our humanity? The fact of the matter is that we're lost and need to be saved."

"Humanism," I replied, "is a dirty word among Christians, and I'm reluctant to use it even though there's such a thing as *Christian humanism*. Though the human race is ethically fallen, the Bible declares that man, even *fallen man*, still bears the image of God, which brings us full circle to where we began. Man, even in his fallen condition, is able to do marvelous things as the steward of God's creation. Since the beginning of time he has been working it and subduing it, as God commanded Adam and his sons to do. And believers and unbelievers alike enjoy the benefits of man's fulfilling the mandate given to Adam."

I then went to my bookcase, took out a book and said to Cindy, "This view of humanism is not an idea peculiar to me. A great defender of the Christian faith, J. I. Packer, has said something along the same line. I have an extra copy of this book, and I'll give it to you if you promise to read it and pass it on to your mother to read." The book was Packer's *Knowing Man*.

"Before I give it to you, I want to read what he says about humanism.

> I am a humanist. In truth, I believe it is only a thoroughgoing Christian who can ever have a right to that name. . . .
>
> What is humanism? Essentially, it is a quest: a quest for full realization of the possibilities of our humanity. We see ourselves as less satisfied, less fulfilled, less developed, less fully expressed, than we might be; we have not yet tasted all that could enrich us, nor yet developed all our creative potential, nor yet made the most of relationships with others, nor yet fully harnessed the powers of the physical world as instruments of our freedom; and we long to enter further into what we see as our human heritage. In this basic sense we are all humanists; our natural self-love, which God implanted in us, makes us so. You would have to say of anyone who had ceased to look for personal enrichment in any of these ways (as alas, broken folk sometimes do) that he or she was hereby lapsing from one dimension of humanness, as if to contract out of the human race.[1]

"CONTRACT OUT OF THE HUMAN RACE"

I told Cindy that this was what her mother was doing and what *she* was in danger of doing. She was turning her back on God-given human resources for health and happiness—resources that originated in her humanity and are a legacy of her first birth. She acted as though the second birth rendered inoperative the first birth.

Part of the problem was that both Cindy and her mother viewed "natural" ability wholly in a spiritual sense—in the sense used in 1 Corinthians 2:14. To them, "natural" equaled "sinful." They didn't understand that the word *natural* is a legitimate description of human nature, which is the image of God. Human nature has the ability to do great and marvelous things because we are the image of God. They were making the mistake of thinking of the human nature and the sin nature as one and the same, never realizing that *Christ* had a human nature but not a sin nature.

I then said to Cindy and Bobby, "I do not think that man has any hope after death without Christ. But because he bears the image of God, he is extraordinarily gifted by God in the here and now. This we must not ignore. Whatever talents he may have as a man, he enjoys because *God* has gifted him. This is the argument of Romans 1 and the reason that eternal condemnation for the man or woman without Christ is just."

A QUESTION OF RESPECT

Cindy took the book reluctantly. I had serious doubts that she would read it, let alone pass it on to her mother. There was an awkward silence until Bobby spoke.

"Do you know what my problem is in this marriage? I'm suffering from Rodney Dangerfield Syndrome."

Cindy's quizzical look indicated that she had never heard of comedian Rodney Dangerfield.

I explained to her, "He is a comedian whose favorite line is, 'I don't get no respect.'" Then I asked Bobby, "You mean you don't get any respect from Cindy?"

"Right," he replied. "And her mother is ten times worse. I refuse to go over to her mother's house anymore."

"What do they do to make you feel their lack of respect?" I asked.

"With Cindy it's her attitude; with her mother, it's her outright hostility and her determination to cram the Bible down my throat. It seems that no matter what I do,

Cindy's attitude is that my actions are nice, but because I'm not a Christian, they somehow have been tainted or spoiled.

"A case in point is something that happened recently in my law firm. We had a client who wanted to bring a civil suit against the general partner of a tax shelter for losses incurred in the tax shelter. His general partner had managed the shelter poorly, and it looked as though there might even be evidence of fraud.

"My partner and I considered the case, but there was not a clear-cut violation of the law. The general partner did not manage the partnership well, but I didn't think we could make a case on his failure to perform on their contract. But there was no question that the client would spend more money on a lawsuit than he would ever recover on his tax shelter.

"I told my partner that I thought the right thing to do was to tell this to our client. But he replied, 'You don't know that for a fact. It's no reason for turning down a lucrative case like this.'

"But the truth of the matter is that my partner knows our client is a wealthy man, that it wouldn't hurt him financially to spend big bucks on a lost cause, and that we'd stand to make a tidy fee. I told my partner this and suggested that he'd get pretty mad if his doctor prescribed unnecessary surgery. He resented the comparison, but I was able to mollify him. After further discussion he agreed to be honest with our client and discourage him from pursuing the case.

"I felt pretty proud of this. It seemed to be a triumph of legal ethics, and I told Cindy as much. Do you know what her response was? Utter indifference! She gave me a response something like, 'That's nice Bobby,' and went on to some other subject.

"It doesn't matter what I do of value in my work. It's as though it's of no worth. I think you put your finger on it when you said that she and her mother have a problem with placing any value on decent human behavior.

"I am respected by my colleagues, by the financial community and even grudgingly, by my partner. But by my wife? Yeah, I feel like Rodney Dangerfield—'I don't get no respect!' "

MAKING THE MARRIAGE WORK

Cindy seemed to understand what Bobby and I were saying, but how would she translate this into marital harmony? She needed to develop a more adequate understanding of the doctrine of man. Because she limited her view of man to his fallen nature and need of salvation, she could see nothing but his need to be saved. Also, she was afraid that if she did agree that unbelievers in general, and Bobby in particular, were capable of decent behavior, this might detract from the fact that they need to be saved. This again was producing in her a negative attitude toward everything Bobby did.

I think Cindy would have responded well to me if it weren't for her mother. Though Cindy had gone away to college and married, in one sense her mother had never let her leave home. Cindy's mother always kept the apron strings securely tied.

But Cindy was part of the problem, too. She never fought for her independence. She never tried to cut the apron strings. As a result, her mother was still an intrusive force in her life. Mother lived close enough to drop in whenever she felt like it, though she never did when Bobby was there. It seemed that she was always there to give Cindy helpful suggestions as to how she should run her house and raise her children. She would come into the house without knocking, go to the baby's room to be sure that he was comfortable, or covered, or fed, or had dry diapers. She would sit for hours in the family room keeping Cindy a captive audience, instructing her how to manage her home, her husband, and her life. And Cindy put up with it.

Bobby had every reason not to like his mother-in-law. Not only had she made it abundantly clear that she felt he as an unbeliever had nothing of value to offer Cindy in marriage, but she also was a busybody and the manager of his household. The tension between the two had little to do with the fact that Bobby was an unbeliever, though his mother-in-law insisted that was the issue. Even if Bobby were a Christian, they still would have had big problems.

Not only would Cindy have to learn how to physically keep her mother out of her house, but she would have to learn to mentally keep her mother out of her marriage by making *Bobby* her confidante. She needed to be talking to *him* about her needs, the details of household management, and the rearing of the children. Bobby was effectively excluded from being a partner in the marriage because Cindy made her mother her confidante.

Though she didn't say it in so many words, Cindy's mother insisted that the only way Cindy would have a Christian home was to exclude Bobby from guidance and decision making. But she was wrong. The only way her home would be a Christian home would be for Cindy to cut her mother's apron strings and put Bobby back in a position of authority and respect as husband and father.

This would require Cindy to confront her mother, something that she didn't have the stomach to do. She accused Bobby of being non-confrontational, but she was just as bad. She would have to stop her mother from poisoning her mind about unbelievers and from putting down Bobby. Cindy had to see Bobby as a creature created in the image of God, able to make some very good decisions about household management, the enrichment of the marriage, and the rearing of the children. As long as Cindy accepted her mother's idea that unbelievers contribute nothing to a Christian home, anything Bobby said automatically would be discounted, no matter how good his suggestion might be.

Cindy still had reservations about her marriage working. "Even if everything you are saying is biblically sound, I think that Bobby and I really have very little in common. And we always will have little in common as long as he is an unbeliever."

Were Cindy's fears justified?

Can a believer and unbeliever have anything in common outside of Christ?

Cindy's question deserved careful examination.

5

Where Is the Common Ground?

Though I had wished Cindy's mother would keep her nose out of her daughter's marriage and quit raising doubts in Cindy's mind, Cindy did have a legitimate question: How could she have anything in common with Bobby as long as he was an unbeliever?

We already saw that believers have nothing in common with the children of Belial—unrestrained unbelievers. Indeed, we are called to separate ourselves from them (2 Cor. 6:14–7:1).

But what about unbelievers who are not unrestrained but decent people? Do we have anything in common with them?

In one sense, there is no common ground—neutral territory, if you will—upon which a believer and unbeliever can discuss their differences. The reason is that there are no neutral facts that can be appealed to, no neutral logic that can be employed, that enable the believer and unbeliever to come to some sort of agreement apart from God. If any scientific evidence is true, it is true because *God* has made it true. Truth is not an entity that exists apart from God. It is He who makes truth what it is—truth! This is the case with both scientific evidence and the laws of logic that enable two people to have a meeting of the minds. From this point of view, the believer and unbeliever have no common ground.

But there is a sense in which we hold common ground with the unbeliever in everything. We as human beings share the same world, whether or not we agree on its origin or on why it functions with order. Cindy and Bobby share this common ground as parents of two lovely children, as owners of a home that they both enjoy, and as people who relish books, music, plays, and museums. Cindy also had reason to be proud of Bobby's professionalism. Even though he didn't acknowledge that the profession of law owed its existence to the God of order, and even though he didn't acknowledge that ethics in law are essential because the God of order is also a holy God, Bobby still was God's instrument of good on the earth. But Cindy managed to spoil what she did have in common with him.

CINDY THE SPOILER

When I saw Cindy and Bobby again, we took up this subject.

"Cindy," I began, "you complain that you and Bobby have nothing in common because you are a believer and he is an unbeliever. But you have much in common."

Then I pointed out to Cindy all the things she had in common with Bobby as a fellow citizen of planet Earth. I reminded her of her children, lovely home, cultural activities, and even of Bobby's profession—all of which were gifts from God of common grace, gifts that they ought to be sharing.

"All of those things are of no value when compared to what God has done for us in Christ," she replied. "In fact, I see Christian women getting wrapped up in all of those things and forgetting what really is important—the message of salvation."

I had to interrupt. "Cindy, you can't separate these things from God's total program. All of these gifts that God gives us are designed to witness to His graciousness and the salvation He offers in Christ. Whenever you put down these things as unimportant and refuse to enjoy them with Bobby, you are keeping Bobby from seeing how gracious God is."

"What do you mean?" Cindy asked.

"There are two important verses of Scripture that have a bearing on what I'm talking about." I opened my Bible and read,

> In the past, he let all nations go their own way. Yet he has not left himself without testimony: He has shown kindness by giving you rain from heaven and crops in their seasons; he provides you with plenty of food and fills your hearts with joy (Acts 14:16, 17).

"Though the Bible is clear that a day of judgment is coming, God witnesses to unbelieving man of His goodness and graciousness by giving even evil men good gifts. In giving these good gifts to unbelieving, unworthy men, God is saying, 'I want you to know that I am a gracious God. See what I have given you. In fact, I love you so much that I want to give you an even greater gift of my grace. I want to give you the gift of reconciliation through my Son, Jesus Christ!' God's graciousness in His creation sets the stage for a witness to His greatest gift of grace, salvation in Christ.

"This is borne out by what Paul says in Romans 2:4:

Or do you show contempt for the riches of his
kindness, tolerance and patience, not realizing that
God's kindness leads you toward repentance?

"Cindy, God's kindness in giving us these marvelous
gifts is calculated to lead unbelieving men to repentance.
By refusing to value these gifts and enjoy them with
Bobby, you actually are standing in the way of God's
leading Bobby to repentance."

I then smiled and said, "Bobby, please don't misun-
derstand the use of the word 'repentance.' I'm not
suggesting that your behavior is bad. In fact, I think your
behavior is a lot better than your mother-in-law's, and she
claims to be a Christian! Repentance means 'to change
your mind.' A change of mind for you would mean that
you accept the idea that you need to be reconciled to God
because you never can be good enough to gain acceptance
on your own, that God is a gracious God, and this
graciousness is not only seen in His creation but in the
greatest act of His grace, the sacrifice of His Son for your
sins. I know you don't like this bloody religion. But just as
the blood of many an American soldier has purchased the
freedom we enjoy in our democracy, so the blood of
Christ offers us eternal freedom from the slavery of sin
and its consequences."

Bobby smiled and said, "You know, even though I
don't believe what you're saying, somehow it sounds a lot
more palatable than what I've been hearing from Cindy
and her mother."

I replied, "Bobby, what I'm hoping for is that God will
so overwhelm you with His goodness that you'll confess
your ingratitude to Him."

Bobby protested, "I'm grateful for a successful law
practice, for two lovely children, and for all the material
things I have."

"Grateful to whom?" I asked. "Yes, you're grateful,
but you don't give gratitude to God. You're grateful to

your ancestors who provided an excellent gene pool for you and your children and to your parents for the way they raised you. But God doesn't get a bit of your gratitude."

Bobby smiled. "You're right."

I dropped the matter there. I just wanted to model a different style of witnessing for Cindy, and I didn't want to do the Holy Spirit's work for Him. Only God could convict Bobby of his ingratitude for God's graciousness.

Cindy was the key. I needed her to see that she was to start living life with gusto and to enjoy, with Bobby, all the good things that God had given them. By speaking highly of Bobby's performance as an attorney, by raising and enjoying their children together, by sharing their lovely home together with friends, by going to concerts and plays and sailing with him *she would be doing God's work*. As a Christian, she would be an ever-present reminder to Bobby that they enjoyed the good life because God is a gracious God. And, perhaps, this graciousness might just lead Bobby to repentance! She didn't have to beat Bobby over the head with the gospel. All she had to do was be grateful to God for His goodness, enjoy it, and be ready to give an answer to Bobby for the hope that she has (1 Peter 3:15). I told her that this is "friendship evangelism."

BECOMING BOBBY'S FRIEND

Cindy was so accustomed to taking an adversarial posture with Bobby that she really didn't know how to go about making him a friend. I introduced her to my Couples Friendship Inventory, not only to evaluate the level of friendship they enjoyed in marriage but also to use it as a tool for improving this dimension of their relationship.[1] (You will find this inventory in the Appendix.)

I began by pointing out that friendship in marriage is a
peer relationship based on common interest and respect
for each other's equality. Cindy needed to see that even
though spiritually they were not equals, *as human beings
they were*. I decided to take Cindy through the inventory
first. I felt that it would help her see what she could do
about the estrangement she felt in the marriage—an
estrangement that she was, in reality, guilty of creating.

"Cindy, the first item on the inventory is, 'I respect
him.' Do you respect Bobby?" I asked.

She hesitated. Finally she said, "If I listen to my
mother, I would have to say no simply because Bobby is
an unbeliever. If I believe what you say, I should see non-
Christians in a different light. I should be able to respect
them even though they're lost. I know you see God at
work in Bobby even though he is an unbeliever. Even
though he takes credit himself for his accomplishments, I
suppose I should realize that God has given him a great
deal of talent."

Bobby smiled and shook his head. I knew he was
thinking, *You people never give up*. But he didn't seem
offended by the blatant attempt to give God the credit for
his talent.

"The second item is, 'I like him as he is.' Cindy do you
like him as he is?" I asked.

"He is the best husband a wife could have," Cindy
replied. "I only wish he were a Christian."

"Let's set that aside for a minute," I suggested. "For
some reason I feel that God will take care of that if you do
your part. I'd like you to value what you *do* have in your
relationship. Bobby *is* a good husband."

Cindy affirmed this, smiling as she glanced over to
Bobby.

"The third item is, 'I could live without him, but my

life would be poorer for it.' How would you reply to that?" I asked Cindy.

"I don't know," she replied. "I guess that I think so much about what it would be like to be married to a Christian, I really don't value what we do have in common. I have this fantasy of studying the Bible, praying with my husband, and having discussions about spiritual things. I miss this in our relationship so much that I guess I take for granted the good things that we do have going for us."

I suggested to Cindy that even if she were married to a Christian man, there is no guarantee her fantasy would come true. I told her that I knew a lot of Christian husbands who not only offer no spiritual companionship to their wives but are not nearly as decent as Bobby is in the other areas of marriage.

Cindy agreed that this was true. In fact, she thought that her fantasy might actually be keeping her from appreciating what she did have in her marriage to Bobby.

I continued the inventory. "The next item is, 'I enjoy sharing what we have in common with others of like mind.' How would you answer that?" I asked.

"That's a tough one," Cindy replied. "I have a problem with the part that says 'with others of like mind.' Bobby and his friends simply don't see things the way I do. How can I share anything with them when we're not like-minded?"

I pointed out to Cindy that she was failing to make an important distinction. "It is true that you are not like-minded on the things of the Spirit of God. Only spiritual people can understand spiritual things (1 Cor. 2:14–15). But you do have a lot in common with unbelievers concerning external things not having to do with the things of the Spirit. When you eat out with your friends, go to the concerts and the theater, you certainly are in agreement over good food, good acting, and good music. You may not agree over *why* these things are good. You know that it is God who provides you with plenty of food and fills your hearts with joy (Acts 14:17). As the occasion permits, you may even have opportunity to give God the glory. But you don't have to spoil a perfectly good time simply because Bobby and his non-Christian friends don't give God thanks for these good things. Leave the convicting work of the Holy Spirit up to the Holy Spirit."

We didn't have enough time to go through all seventeen items on the inventory in that session. In fact, it would take several sessions to go through it and discuss the fact that friendship with Bobby was possible.

These sessions began to help Cindy change her attitude toward Bobby once again. She began to show more respect for him, genuine admiration for his skill as an attorney, and great confidence in him as the father of their children. She also began to enjoy more the time she spent with him and his friends. She saw that she didn't have to look at life as they did in order to enjoy the things they had in common.

Bobby began to change, too. He was less defensive and belligerent about Christianity. He began to feel Cindy's acceptance, and her acceptance was genuine because she was able to separate Bobby-the-man-made-in-God's-image from Bobby-the-enemy-of-God, dead in trespasses and sins. This had a strange effect on Bobby.

Privately, I shared with Cindy what I thought was happening. Bobby knew that now she was more accepting and loving because she saw him as a creature made in God's image and worthy of admiration because God was at work in him. Even though he wanted to take the credit for being a successful attorney, a good father, and a good husband, Cindy's respect and appreciation was an ever-present reminder that he ought to be giving the credit to God. At this time, though, Bobby was unresponsive to God's grace.

Something very significant happened as a result of their learning to live together successfully as believer and unbeliever. They were able to see more clearly the major problems in their marriage that had been obscured by Cindy's unhappiness over Bobby's unbelief.

They discovered that if their marriage was to succeed, they had to come to terms with three serious problems.

6

Is There a Reason for Hope?

Cindy was like many Christians who are married to non-Christians. She had clung to the belief that her unhappiness in marriage was due to the fact that Bobby was an unbeliever and that she would never have happiness until he accepted Christ as his Savior.

BEYOND UNBELIEF

Finally Cindy was able to accept the idea that happiness in marriage was possible, even though Bobby was not a Christian. She saw that she could respect him and enjoy a great deal in common with him, even though he was an unbeliever. She also realized that as long as she clung to the notion that the basic problem with the marriage was Bobby's unbelief, she was able to ignore the three problems that had far more impact on their everyday lives than Bobby's unbelief: their style of communication, Bobby's nice-guy facade, and Cindy's mother.

Improving Communication

One of my long-range goals with Bobby and Cindy was to help them improve their style of communication.

Unless a couple can talk about their problems constructively, they will not be able to identify their problems or
solve them. I summarized the two most important
guidelines they needed to learn about communication.

Communication is first and foremost to achieve
understanding rather than agreement. Secondly, all
communication is to be non-attacking and non-defen-
sive.

Cindy and Bobby had a problem that most couples
have, whether or not they are Christians. Whenever they
discussed something that they had a difference of opinion
about, they tried to prove each other wrong and themselves right. It was not Bobby's unbelief that made
communication difficult, but their destructive style of
communication. Fortunately, both were willing to correct
it.[1]

Bobby's Nice-Guy Facade

The second thing we needed to work on was Bobby's
nice-guy facade. Being nice is both a Christian and
cultural ideal so you may wonder why this should be
tampered with. Because Bobby was more than nice. He
had such an aversion to hostility that he was not able to
see malice or evil intent in people when he should.
Consequently, he often was used and abused by people,
something that he readily accepted, but left Cindy feeling
terribly insecure. Bobby always would be a nice guy, but
my task was to help him become a more balanced person
in the expression of his personality.

Cindy's Mother

Perhaps the biggest impediment to happiness in this
marriage was Cindy's mother and Cindy's unwillingness

to confront her mother's intrusion into their marriage and her constant putdowns of Bobby. Bobby needed both the respect and the loyalty of his wife. Cindy had to see that she could and should take a stand with her unbelieving husband against her Christian mother. If a marriage is to work, both the husband and wife must leave father and mother and establish a oneness with their mate (Gen. 2:24).

Cindy's respect for and loyalty to Bobby would solve another problem—Bobby's tendency to undercut the children's faith. Bobby admitted that he did this because he was tired of Cindy's putdowns as well as her mother's telling him how wrong he was about everything. He used the children as a way to get back, a forum for his own point of view. He admitted that this was destructive and was willing not to undercut what they were being taught at church.

"They don't have to believe as I do," he said. "I just want them to respect the opinions of other people. I don't think a person has to be a bigot to be a Christian."

Cindy was satisfied with this. She didn't want her children to be bigots either. She was beginning to see that there were other problems in her marriage besides her husband's unbelief, problems that were more destructive. She began to be hopeful about the future of her marriage as she and Bobby were able to talk more constructively about those other problems. Though she prayed constantly for Bobby's salvation, she was willing to accept the idea that she *could* have a happy marriage while she waited for it to happen. By being a more winsome wife, Cindy would no doubt be a more effective witness to her husband.

THE GOD WHO IS IN CHARGE

But there was another reason for hope that Cindy had. I spent some time with her alone, dealing with what she felt was an unforgivable sin: her deliberate marriage to an unbeliever. She felt that her disobedience to God put her in the place where she was doomed to an unhappy marriage for the rest of her life.

I pointed out that nowhere does Scripture declare marriage to an unbeliever to be sin. We are not to marry unrestrained idolators. There is a difference. As had been previously discussed, Moses' and Hosea's marriages to unbelievers bore out my contention that the unequal yoke of 2 Corinthians 6 does not have to do with marriage to a non-Christian but refers to binding relationships, in marriage or otherwise, with *practicing idolaters*, the children of Belial who show their allegiance to Satan by their unrestrained immorality. Cindy's marriage to an unbeliever may not have been a good choice, just as Moses' marriage to Zipporah was not a good choice. But Cindy needed to know that God is in control of her life *in spite of her not-so-good choices*.

"Do you have any biblical support for that statement?" Cindy asked.

"You're acquainted with Romans 8:28?" I asked.

"Yes, God works all things for the good of those who love Him."

"You're leaving something out," I replied. "Those who love Him are identified as those 'who have been called according to His purpose.' Cindy, God has a purpose for your life. It is to save you and conform you to the image of Christ. This is not something you can take or leave. This is not something that an unwise choice can thwart. Do you think for a moment that because you married Bobby, an unbeliever, that somehow you have thwarted the purpose of an all-powerful, sovereign God? If you could, then I don't think much of your god.

"This is reinforced by Ephesians 1:11–14, where Paul

says that you are saved and kept, not because of what you have done, but because of what God has determined to do in your life.

"Cindy, what God has begun, He intends to carry out. Romans 8:28 is true because of what is said in the verses that follow.

> For those God foreknew he also predestined to be conformed to the likeness of his Son, that he might be the firstborn among many brothers. And those he predestined, he also called; those he called, he also justified; those he justified, he also glorified (Rom. 8:29–30).

"Many of us make bad choices in life. Some of us do downright stupid things. But our bad choices and our stupidity cannot thwart the purpose of an all-powerful, sovereign God. If they could, then God would not be all-powerful and sovereign.

"It may be that God is using your decision to marry Bobby to bring you back to Him and to show you that He does love you. Remember how you felt when you were in college and decided to marry Bobby? Remember you felt that God didn't love you? He knew that you needed a decent husband, but He didn't come through. Remember when you decided that you were going to take matters into your own hands—and you did? Do you think that this mere human being, Cindy, can thwart God's determination to conform you to the likeness of His Son?

"When we doubt that God has our best interest at heart, He sometimes deals with us by letting us have our own way. This is seen in the history of Israel again and again. When we insist on our own way and get it, we usually make a mess of things. And sometimes, it is only by making a mess of things that we are able to admit we don't do such a good job at running our lives.

"This is what parents do with self-willed teenagers to help them grow up and learn to exercise mature judgment. Though they don't permit the teen to destroy himself, and though they don't disinherit him from the family for his self-will, parents do permit him a great deal of freedom of choice that becomes a tremendous learning experience.

"Cindy, at one time you were turned off by Christians and wanted nothing to do with them. By permitting you to marry an unbeliever, God brought you back to Him. And not only that, as a result of the spiritual dryness you have experienced in your marriage to Bobby, you have developed an unquenchable thirst for spiritual things."

Cindy laid her head back on the headrest of the chair and smiled. She was silent for a long time. Finally, she spoke.

"It is quite remarkable, isn't it? He *is* in control of my life."

"Not only that," I replied, "Paul says, 'If God is for us, who can be against us?'" (Rom. 8:31). Then I read the rest of Romans 8. About halfway through Cindy began to cry.

"What are the tears about?" I asked.

"That part you read, 'Who is he that condemns?' (Rom. 8:34). I guess that's been my biggest problem— self-condemnation—and my mother has done a good job of reinforcing it. I guess I felt that I had ruined my life by marrying Bobby and that I would never be happy unless he became a Christian. Because of my guilt I punished myself, I let my mother run my life, and I tried to convert Bobby by keeping after him all the time. I guess it's time I stop trying to do things my way and leave Bobby's salvation to God."

CONTENTMENT AT LAST

Bobby is not yet a Christian, but he and Cindy are experiencing a contentment in their marriage that they never had before. They have become fast friends and are communicating. Bobby is coming to terms with his nice-guy facade and, much to the distress of Cindy's mother, Cindy has cut the apron strings.

Whether or not Bobby will ever receive Christ as his Savior, I don't know. But this much I do know: God has left a testimony for Bobby. His kindness has been evident, particularly in Bobby's marriage. Cindy and I are hoping that God's kindness to Bobby will lead him to repentance.

WHEN YOUR MATE IS NOT SO NICE

One of the things that made it easy for Cindy to accept her marriage to an unsaved husband was that Bobby was a nice person. He was easy to live with, though sometimes Cindy felt that he was *too* nice.

But what do you do when your mate is not so nice? Perhaps your husband is a bully. Maybe your wife is a shrew. What then?

It's a mistake to believe that salvation will instantaneously change behavior. Though it is true that we become a new creation in Christ when we're saved, if we don't grow into mature Christians, we will carry our ugly behavior into the Christian life and be ugly Christians. We may even *justify* our ugly behavior on biblical grounds.

A common problem I have with angry, abusive Christian husbands is that they use Ephesians 5:22–33 and the concept of the headship of the husband to abuse verbally, and sometimes physically, their wives who "get out of line." Sometimes this is used in reverse by the shrewish wife who is perpetually angry and resentful toward her husband for not taking leadership in the marriage.

These people are difficult to live with, whether or not they are Christians. And often when they do become Christians, they resist God's determination to conform them to the image of Christ. Much of the trouble they experience as Christians is stubbornness and self-will that God must break.

> Salvation of a lost mate is not the panacea for an unhappy or troubled marriage. If that mate makes Christ his Savior but not his Lord, the marriage will still be in trouble. Your mate must understand that salvation is not just a ticket to heaven but a life revolutionized by the Savior. It may be that your mate's salvation is delayed because God knows that your mate's self-will must be broken.

Are you willing to let God deal with that rebellious mate? It may be that he doesn't come to the end of his rope because you keep him from facing the consequences of his behavior. You keep fixing the damage he does; you keep bailing him out of the mess he makes of his life. And you usually do it so *you* will survive. But that doesn't help your mate. For further reading about physical, psychological, and verbal abuse, read Holly Wagner Green's *Turning Fear to Hope* (Grand Rapids: Zondervan Publishing House, 1989). In this book, she answers questions such as "How is it possible for a man to be Christian and yet abuse his wife?"; "Should a woman suffer abuse 'for the Lord's sake'?"; "Is it wrong for a Christian wife to try to escape from an abusive husband?"; "What does it mean to be a submissive wife?" *Turning Fear to Hope* offers important, vital suggestions on what you should do as a Christian, right now. When you read it, you'll uncover the secret of turning your fear into hope.

God wants to do something about your difficult mate, but the first step may be for YOU to get out of HIS way.

COUPLES
FRIENDSHIP
INVENTORY

The purpose of this inventory is to give couples an opportunity to discuss the quality of their friendship in marriage. Spouses should take the inventory and compare their responses. Do they differ in their responses? If so, why?

Under each statement is an explanation of what is meant. Though the masculine pronoun is used in the explanation, the feminine pronoun should be understood when the husband is evaluating his wife. Each statement should be responded to on a scale of 1 to 5—5 indicating that the quality is definitely found in the relationship, and 1 that it definitely is not found. A 3 response is neither yes or no. A 2 or 4 gives the respondent an opportunity to indicate a lesser degree of yes or no.

The total scores will give an indication of the strength or weakness of your friendship.

                                              No   Yes
1. I respect him/her.   1 2 3 4 5

Even though he is an individual in his own right, I feel an
affinity with him. He may be unlike me, but even so, I feel
that I complement him. We share common ideas, ideals,
and activities, and I respect his approach to the things we
have in common.

2. I like him/her as he/she is.   1 2 3 4 5

He doesn't have to be like me in order for me to like him. I
feel a common bond with him and admire the way he
thinks and acts.

3. I could live without him, but my life would be poorer
   for it.   1 2 3 4 5

One of the things I value about him is the richness he
brings to my life. I could get along without him if I had to,
but knowing him brings pleasure to my life. His value to
me is more than just emotional or physical survival.

4. I enjoy sharing what we have in common with others
   of like mind.   1 2 3 4 5

Though my relationship with him may be exclusive as far
as emotional and sexual intimacy are concerned, the two
of us enjoy like-minded people who share the ideas and
ideals we hold in common.

5. If we were not married, we would still share a lot of
   the same ideas, ideals, and activities. 1 2 3 4 5

Our marriage involves a number of things such as
emotional intimacy and sexual attraction. But we would
still be friends even if not married because of the ideas,
ideals, and activities we have in common.

6. I respect him/her even when he/she does things that
   upset or annoy me.   1 2 3 4 5

Our relationship is not based on my comfort or pleasure but on a common bond and a view of life that surpasses personal gratification.

7. I know him/her well enough that I can anticipate what his/her words or behavior will be in most circumstances. 1 2 3 4 5

Because we share common ideas and ideals, I can tell how he will react in most circumstances. That reaction will be consistent with the way I know he looks at life.

8. It's easy to turn a blind eye to his/her faults.

1 2 3 4 5

Because I feel that he is committed to our common ideas, ideals, and interests, it's easy to overlook minor and occasional failures to live up to them.

9. I want what is best for him/her. 1 2 3 4 5

My relationship with him is not based solely on the gratification of my own needs, but also on a sincere desire to have him experience what is best for him.

10. I care enough to let him/her go, even give him/her up.
1 2 3 4 5

I am willing to sacrifice my own needs if letting him go is in his best interest.

11. My respect for him/her is *not* based on his/her accomplishments. 1 2 3 4 5

The basis of my respect is his fidelity to the ideas and ideals that we hold in common. He could achieve less and still be my friend.

12. I know he/she is a kindred spirit even though I may not be assured frequently that he/she is. 1 2 3 4 5

Because our kindred spirit is felt and demonstrated in many little ways, I don't need frequent assurance that it's there.

13. He/she seems to bring out the best in me.   1 2 3 4 5

Because we share common ideas and ideals, when I am with him I find that my thinking about and expression of these things are stimulated by him.

14. I feel that we stand together against the view of outsiders.   1 2 3 4 5

Views of others that run contrary to the way we think tend to unite, rather than divide us.

15. I can be both strong and weak with him/her.

1 2 3 4 5

Because we have mutual respect for each other, strength is not threatening nor is weakness despised.

16. My giving to him/her is characterized by freedom and willingness and not grudging sacrifice.   1 2 3 4 5

Because I want what is best for him, I am willing to give freely without thought of its cost to me.

17. My relationship with him/her is characterized by trust.   1 2 3 4 5

I believe that his actions have my best interests at heart, and they are selfless in motive, and therefore I am able to trust him.

Now total your scores and compare them with this table:

Very good friendship	73–85
Good friendship	60–72
Needs work	47–59
Poor friendship	34–46
Very poor friendship	17–33

VALUES EXERCISE

Because God has created the world and the human race, we are subject to rules that reflect His holiness. We call these "laws of nature." Whether or not a person believes in God, the success of his life will depend on how well he understands the laws by which nature and society function and how careful he is to observe these rules.

"Values" are social principles, goals, and standards we adopt to help us follow these God-given laws of nature. As a couple, how similar are your values? The following exercise is designed to help you see how close or far apart you are in your ability to work together for the common good of your family. Husbands and wives should read the following and discuss what they would say or do.

1. **You have returned from the store with your child and discover that while you were there he stole some candy. What do you tell your child? What do you do about it?**

2. **Your sixteen-year-old has made it clear that he/she sees nothing wrong with having sexual intercourse with "someone you love." What do you tell your teen? What do you do about the danger of pregnancy and disease?**

3. Your child is now twenty-two and is living with his/her girlfriend/boyfriend without the benefit of marriage. They are going to visit you over the Christmas holidays and they expect to share the same bed together. What do you tell them? What do you do?

4. You have a charge account at a large department store and purchase a washing machine, which you charge to your account. After several months you realize that the charge never appeared on your monthly charge account statement. What do you do?

5. You don't want any more children because of financial hardship, but you discover that another child is on the way. What do you do?

6. You find yourself strongly attracted to someone other than your mate, and you frequently fantasize what it would be like to have sexual relations with that person. What do you do about it?

7. You discover that your sixteen-year-old is drinking on a regular basis, several times a week. What do you tell him? What do you do?

8. You want to tithe your joint income to the church. How does your mate feel about it? Would he/she agree to do it?

9. Your son wants to go to seminary and become a minister. How does your mate feel about it? Would he/she agree to it?

10. You would like to have a Bible study in your home. How does your mate feel about it? Would he/she agree to it?

NOTES

Introduction

1. Carolyn J. Holmgrain, "Marriage Declines Among Young Catholics," *AAMFT* (American Association for Marriage and Family Therapy) *News* (July/August 1985): p. 20.
2. Ibid.

Chapter 1

1. Andre Bustanoby, *Being a Success at Who You Are* (Grand Rapids: Zondervan Publishing House, 1985), p. 11.

Chapter 2

1. Gustave F. Oehler, *Old Testament Theology* (Grand Rapids: Zondervan Publishing House, 1983), p. 180.
2. Carl F. Keil, *Ezra, Nehemiah, Esther* (Grand Rapids: Eerdmans, n.d.), p. 110.
3. Carl F. Keil, *Minor Prophets, II* (Grand Rapids: Eerdmans, n.d.), p. 499.
4. James Orr, ed., *International Standard Bible Encyclopedia*, 3 vols. (Grand Rapids: Eerdmans, 1952), III:1246.

Chapter 4

1. J. I. Packer, *Knowing Man* (Westchester, Ill.: Cornerstone Books, 1980), pp. 11–12.

Chapter 5

1. Andre Bustanoby, *Can Men and Women Be Just Friends?* (Grand Rapids: Zondervan Publishing House, 1985), pp. 112–16.

Chapter 6

1. For more on communication, see my book, *Just Talk to Me* (Grand Rapids: Zondervan Publishing House, 1981).